DATE DUE

AUG 4 78	FEB 25 '80	JUL 9 '80	NO 23 '95
AUG 18 78	MAR 2 7 '80	OCT 11 84	7 7
AUG 28 78	MAY 1 7 '80	APR 7 88	
OCT 11 78	JUL 4 '80	SEP 26 '86	
NOV 8 78	DEC 2 '80	NOV 20 86	
NOV 28 78	JAN 3 '81	DEC 3 86	
DEC 9 78	JAN 14 '81	APR 12 '88	
DEC 12 78	AUG 18 '82	MAY 7 '88	
JAN 18 79	DEC 1 '82	MAY 7 '88	
FEB 1 79	JAN 12 '83	JUL 11 88	
FEB 8 '79	FEB 1 '83	AUG 17 88	
APR 24 79	MAY 19 '83	OCT 15 '88	
JUL 13 79	MAY 31 '83	DEC 1 '88	
JUL 19 79	JUL 2 '83	NOV 27 88	
AUG 9 79	SEP 6 '83	FEB 8 '93	
SEP 22 79	APR 2 84	MR 25 '94	
FEB 8 80	JUN 15 84	MY 6 '95	

Cornzapoppin'!

POPCORN RECIPES AND PARTY IDEAS
FOR ALL OCCASIONS

Barbara Williams

CORNZAPOPPIN'!

Popcorn Recipes and Party Ideas for All Occasions

Photographs by ROYCE L. BAIR

Holt, Rinehart and Winston / NEW YORK

The author wishes to thank Wrede H. Smith, president of the American Pop Corn Company, for his unstinting cooperation in the preparation of this book.

FOR NONIE

10 9 8 7 6 5 4 3 2 1

Library of Congress Cataloging in Publication Data

Williams, Barbara.

Cornzapoppin'!
Includes index.
SUMMARY: A guide to the history, growing, buying, storing, popping,
and flavoring of popcorn accompanies special recipe,
decorating, and party ideas for occasions throughout the year.
1. Pop-corn—Juvenile literature. [1. Popcorn.
2. Handicraft] I. Title
TX799.W54   1976   641.3'31'5   75-28329
ISBN 0-03-014366-7

Contents

JANUARY

FEBRUARY

MAY

JUNE

JULY

GIFTS FOR SPECIAL OCCASIONS

Cornzapoppin'!

POPCORN RECIPES AND PARTY IDEAS
FOR ALL OCCASIONS

1 / OUR WONDERFUL GIFT
FROM THE INDIANS

Many people assume that popcorn is regular sweet corn which has been treated in some way to make it pop. Actually, there are three main varieties of corn—sweet corn, which is the kind you eat as a vegetable for dinner; field corn, which is the kind grown as feed for hogs and cattle; and popcorn, which is the favorite snack food of most Americans. Of the three kinds of corn, popcorn is the only one which bursts into a delicious white morsel when exposed to high heat. Scientists assume that the popping process results from a combination of the hard shell and the internal moisture of the popcorn kernel.

Most of the world's popcorn is grown in the Midwestern part of the United States—principally in Nebraska, Iowa, and Indiana, where it can get mighty hot in the summer. Old-timers tell of one particular summer when it got so hot the corn in the fields started popping right off the stalks. The cows and pigs thought it was a snow blizzard and they lay down and froze to death.

Tragedies like that don't happen very often, however. Popcorn is usually associated with happy events like circuses, movies, baseball games, birthdays, Christmas, Halloween, and family occasions around the television set. Americans love popcorn. It is cheaper than candy, less fattening than cookies, easier to prepare than cake, sturdier than ice cream, and more American than apple pie.

Popcorn, in fact, is the oldest truly American confection.

Archaeologists claim that popcorn was the first crop ever grown by the American Indians. The Indians knew about popcorn even before they discovered sweet corn. For nearly six thousand years—long before the time of Jesus or even Confucius—Indians have been popping, eating, and even wearing the tasty white flowers which burst mysteriously from hard kernels. When Columbus landed in the West Indies in 1492, he encountered Indians selling jewelry made of popcorn. A few years later Cortez invaded Mexico and found the Aztecs using popcorn ornaments in their religious ceremonies. But of course, as the Indians knew, the best use for popcorn is to eat it.

The Indians had no butter, but they enjoyed eating popcorn anyway. They also had no electric corn poppers, no gas ranges, not even any cast-iron skillets. But they developed several methods of popping corn nonetheless. The easiest method was to insert the end of a long stick in an ear of popcorn and hold it over the fire. Occasionally the kernels would pop off the cob and into the fire, the way we sometimes lose our wieners and marshmallows. But the Indians seemed to like this method; many of them kept on using it even after electricity was discovered.

Another way they popped corn was to throw loose kernels directly into the fire. When the heat of the fire caused the kernels to burst, the popped corn would usually fly right out of the fire and onto the ground where it could be picked up. This method caused a good deal of needless scampering and bending, so eventually many Indian tribes adopted the more practical hot sand method of popping corn. These tribes would pour a layer of sand into a large clay vessel and then put the vessel over the fire until the sand became very hot. Then they would remove the vessel, pour some kernels of popcorn into the hot sand, and stir the sand with a long stick. As the kernels popped, they would spring to the surface for easy removal.

The Indians were generous in teaching the white men all

they knew about popcorn. According to one legend, an Indian named Quadequina, the brother of the great Iroquois chief Massasoit, caused more excitement than the turkey at the Pilgrims' first Thanksgiving dinner. He brought a deerskin full of popped corn to the feast, poured it out on the table, and invited everyone to dive in.

Apparently the Pilgrims were happy to oblige, for soon the colonial women were serving their families "puffed" corn breakfast cereal with sugar and cream. Meanwhile the men were devising better and better implements with which to pop the intriguing kernels. Eventually they developed the mesh shaker—a contrivance which often wearied the person on the other end of the long handle, for the operator had to shake the kernels constantly to keep them from burning. About 1930, a new type of family-sized corn popper was invented. This implement plugged into an electric outlet but still required constant manual rotation of the kernels by means of a handle on the top of the device. Not for another ten years or so did popcorn lovers discover that the kernels needed little or no rotation if oil was added to the bottom of the cooking implement. After World War II the hand cranks disappeared from family-sized electric corn poppers.

Twice during America's history have popcorn sales taken a sudden rise. The first time was during the Depression of the 1930s when Americans realized how inexpensive popcorn is in relation to other confections. Inventors of commercial corn poppers began installing their machines in theater lob-lobbies, and the popcorn and movie industries developed together.

After World War II, popcorn sales again made a sudden rise—this time by an astonishing 500 per cent! A survey conducted among housewives proved the reason to be the new invention of television. As families started buying television sets, they were changing their life-styles—staying home more and eating popcorn as they watched their screens.

Despite how delicious and inexpensive it is, popcorn is not really popular today in countries other than the United States, Canada, and Mexico. Although small amounts are consumed in Australia and South Africa, popcorn seems to be a confection which only Americans enjoy regularly.

2 / HOW YOU CAN GROW POPCORN FOR PLEASURE AND PROFIT

If you have a few spare feet of fertile soil in a sunny back yard, you may want to try growing your own popcorn patch. A tiny plot 4′ x 8′ should yield about 5 quarts of kernels. Since popcorn increases approximately thirty-two times in volume from kernel to morsel, you'll get 160 quarts of popped corn, which is almost enough for every single recipe, decoration, and favor described in this book. If you can double the size of your plot to 8′ x 8′, you'll have enough for your own needs plus extra corn to sell to neighbors and friends.

Like sweet corn, popcorn requires lots of sunshine and good drainage. It's also a thirsty crop. Some folks in Missouri recall the summer their corn got so thirsty the roots shot down into the earth and drained the Mississippi River so dry a cat could walk across the riverbed. Even if you don't believe that story, don't plant popcorn unless you have a good hose handy and plan to use it.

In most parts of the country late May and early June are the corn-planting months. Choose a spot some distance away from your sweet corn, if you're growing some. The cross-pollination won't harm the popcorn too much, but it may cause the sweet corn to develop hard, unchewable kernels among the tender ones.

You can buy popcorn seed for planting from your local nurseryman, or you can send away for it to a mail-order seed company like the ones listed at the end of this chapter. In addition to the White Hulless and Yellow Hulless varieties of popcorn usually sold by commercial packagers, there are many kinds of popcorn you may choose for your own garden.

17

Strawberry is the smallest variety. It gets its name from the color of its kernels and the shape of its ears. Calico (or Rainbow) popcorn has multicolored ears with white, yellow, blue, and red kernels. It pops into white fluff, however, as does the more familiar Black variety. Dynamite and Snowpuff are among the largest varieties of popcorn. Check with your nurseryman to see what grows best in your part of the country.

Spade the soil deeply and work in 40 pounds of steer manure or commercial fertilizer to an area of 1,000 square feet. You'll need at least three rows of popcorn for proper pollination. Set them 2 feet apart, and mark them with taut string between pegs hammered into the ground. Along the string make a shallow furrow about 1 inch deep. Then sow three or four kernels together at intervals about 15 inches apart and cover with soil. When the plants reach 6 to 8 inches, thin them down to one stalk for every 15 inches and work another 40 pounds of fertilizer into the soil.

Hoe your popcorn patch frequently to keep down weeds, but don't remove suckers at the bases of the stalks. And don't be in a hurry to harvest your crop. Unlike sweet corn, popcorn is not ready to be picked until the husks and leaves are brown and dry. The kernels themselves should be hard, with no milk seeping out. Test several ears with your thumbnail before picking any.

After harvesting your corn you must let it dry further—usually a month or more—before removing the kernels from the ears. Lay the popcorn out on newspapers in a warm, dry room, and don't try to hurry the drying process with artificial heat or you will ruin both the expansion and the flavor of your popped corn.

After two or three weeks start testing your popcorn at regular intervals to see if it has dried sufficiently. Place two or three kernels in a hot skillet with a thin layer of cooking oil on the bottom and a lid on top. The kernels should explode when they reach an internal temperature of 400°. If you hear them burst up against the lid of the pan in three or four minutes, your popcorn is ready for storage.

Remove the husks from your corn and peel off the hard kernels, with your thumbs, from the tops of the ears downward. Pour the corn into tightly covered plastic containers or Mason jars, keeping one jar in your refrigerator for current use. The ideal storage place for the remaining popcorn is your freezer, if you have one. If you don't, a cool basement or root cellar works nearly as well.

Popcorn may not grow in your part of the country if your summer season is short or if your soil is barren, but you can still enjoy the pleasure of popping, flavoring, and eating this delicious snack food.

Mail Order Seed Companies
W. Atlee Burpee Co., Box 748,
Riverside, California 92502

Gill Bros. Seed Co., Box 16128,
Midway Station, Portland, Oregon 97216

3 / BUYING, STORING, POPPING, AND FLAVORING POPCORN

Buying the Corn

Nearly every grocery store in America sells commercially packaged corn for popping. If you can't find it, ask the manager.

While popping corn is half the fun, you may want to purchase corn that is already popped if you are flavoring it for a very large group of people. Check the yellow pages of your telephone book under "Popcorn" for retail stores that sell unflavored popped corn.

Storing the Unpopped Kernels

Popcorn kernels should always be kept in a tightly covered plastic or glass container and stored in a cool, damp place. Your refrigerator is the ideal storage place for an opened package. Your freezer is the ideal place for unopened packages.

Restoring the Pop

When an opened container of popcorn loses its zip, you can usually restore its popping ability. Pour the kernels into a jar or plastic container large enough so that the kernels take up no more than three fourths of the room and add 2 tablespoons of water for each pound of popcorn. Cover the jar tightly, shake it vigorously, and store overnight in the refrigerator. The next day test three or four kernels in a hot skillet with a thin layer of cooking oil on the bottom and a lid on the top. If the kernels still don't pop, repeat the process.

Utensils

Many recipes in this book call for two long-handled spoons, a roasting pan, a double boiler, a large bowl and a heavy metal pot such as a cast-iron pressure cooker. Utensils and/or non-food items required for a given dish appear at the start of each recipe.

Popping the Corn

If you have an electric corn popper, read the instructions that came with it and observe them carefully.

An electric popper isn't necessary, however—not since popcorn-loving Americans discovered how easy it is to pop corn in a pan if you use cooking oil.

Here are the steps:

1. Heat an empty 3-quart saucepan on your range at high setting about 3 minutes.

2. Add enough cooking oil to cover the bottom of the pan (about ¼ cup) and reduce the heat to medium high.

3. Put 2 kernels of popcorn in the oil. When these pop, pour in enough corn to cover the bottom of the pan (no more than ½ cup).

4. Reduce heat to medium low and place a lid on the pan, leaving a crack for steam to escape.

5. Shake pan gently until all popping stops. Remove from heat and empty the popped corn into a large bowl.

6. Choose one of the recipes from the following pages, prepare the popped corn accordingly, and invite the gang over.

Flavoring the Corn

Most Americans like their popcorn flavored either with butter (plus salt or other tart seasonings) or sugar. The butter method is usually easier because the butter is simply melted, not cooked by complicated procedures as are most sugared popcorn recipes. Buttered popcorn is also cheaper and less harmful to your teeth than most kinds of sugared popcorn.

Although they are delicious, sugared popcorn recipes are often difficult to prepare because they require careful timing during the cooking process. Many of the sugared popcorn recipes in this book seem to expect you to be an octopus . . . asking you to warm your popped corn in the oven, to stir your syrup constantly, and to test your syrup *all at the same time!* This isn't easy, even for an experienced cook. To get around the problem, and also for added sociability, you may want to invite a friend to help you stir while you do the other things. If you decide to work alone, you will have to stir with one hand and test the syrup with the other.

Whether you make buttered popcorn or sugared popcorn, your recipe will taste much better if you mix the flavoring through the popped corn very carefully. Mixing procedures are described below.

Testing the Syrup for Sugared Popcorn Recipes

When water and sugar are boiled together, they form a thick liquid, or syrup. The longer they boil, the thicker the syrup becomes. Most candy (and popcorn) recipes depend upon the thickness of this syrup, so cookbooks will tell you to cook a syrup recipe to the soft ball, firm ball, or crack stage. All the recipes in this book require either a soft ball or a firm ball because syrup which has reached the crack stage is too stiff to mix evenly through popcorn.

To test the syrup, fill a china or glass cup half full with cool water. Drop about ¼ teaspoonful (don't waste your syrup by using too much) of the syrup into the water and work it together with your fingers, into a ball.

22

Soft ball stage: syrup will hold together in a genuine round ball—not just a clump—but will gradually lose its shape when removed from the cool water and placed on a flat surface.

Firm ball stage: syrup will hold together in a firm ball which clicks slightly and will not stick when it is tapped against the side of the cup. It will also retain its shape when removed from the cool water and placed on a flat surface.

Crack stage: syrup will separate into threads when it hits the cool water. It will be too stiff to form into a smooth ball and will make a distinct noise when tapped against the side of the cup.

Mixing the Syrup (or Butter) Through Your Popped Corn

Place the popped corn in a roasting pan or other heat-proof container sufficiently large that the corn takes up no more than one third of the space. The sides should be at least 4 inches high. (Most kitchenware stores sell huge "throwaway" roasting pans for about $1.00. These are too lightweight to be practical as roasting pans but are ideal for mixing popcorn. They are easily washed and stored.)

Your syrup will mix more evenly through popcorn which is slightly warm, so place the already popped corn in a slow oven (200°) while you cook your syrup.

Pour the hot syrup over the corn. With a long-handled spoon *in each hand,* work from the outsides of the mixing pan toward the center, lifting the popcorn and then dropping it gently back into the center of the pan. *Count at least 200 strokes.*

JANUARY

New Year's Day

Turn over a new leaf and treat yourself and your friends to more popcorn this year. You can start with a big bowlful of hot buttered popcorn and a tureen of homemade corn soup with popcorn flowerets bobbing on the top.

BUTTERED POPCORN

Everyone's favorite is hot buttered popcorn seasoned with salt. More than 200 million dollars' worth of this simple but nutritious snack food is sold every year *in movie theaters alone!*

Non-food items you will need: two long-handled spoons, roasting pan.

1. Read "Mixing the Syrup (or Butter) Through Your Popped Corn," in Chapter 3.

2. In a large pan, place

   • 6 quarts (24 cups) popped corn

3. Melt on top of stove over low heat

   • ¾ cup (1½ sticks) butter

4. Measure

   • 2 teaspoons salt

5. Pour butter and salt over popped corn and mix well.

Yield: serves 30 dainty snackers or 8–10 hungry ones

HOMEMADE CORN SOUP

This recipe calls for an electric blender, but you can garnish any creamy white soup, such as New England clam showder, with popcorn flowerets for the same attractive effect.

You will probably want to double or triple this recipe, but most blenders are so small that you can mix only one recipe at a time.

Non-food items you will need: food blender, double boiler, strainer, soup tureen.

1. Place in blender

- 1 16-oz. can (2 cups) creamed corn
- ¾ cup evaporated milk
- ¾ cup homogenized milk
- ½ teaspoon salt
- ¼ teaspoon onion salt
- ⅛ teaspoon pepper

2. Blend at high speed for 4 minutes.
3. Put water in bottom of double boiler and heat on stove.
4. Pour corn mixture through strainer into top of double boiler.
5. Add

- 1 tablespoon butter

6. Heat until very warm.
7. Pour hot soup into tureen and garnish with

- 1 cup popped corn
- 2 teaspoons grated parsley

Yield: 4 servings

January Birthday Treat

CORN BALL FONDUE

You've tried meat fondue and fruit fondue, but if you've never dunked popcorn in a fondue pot, this recipe will surprise and delight you. Use it to celebrate a January birthday or some other snowy-day occasion.

Most variety stores and houseware departments of large department stores sell wooden fondue picks appropriate for this recipe. Not to be confused with the heavier wooden dowels discussed later in the book, wooden fondue picks are about the thickness of toothpicks but four or five times as long. If your store doesn't have them, you can use plastic or wooden toothpicks instead.

Non-food items you will need: two long-handled spoons, roasting pan, wooden fondue picks, heavy pan, large bowl, double boiler, electric or hand mixer, fondue pot.

The Corn Balls for Dunking

1. Set aside

   • wooden fondue picks (at least 50)

2. Read "Testing the Syrup for Sugared Popcorn Recipes," in Chapter 3.
3. Read "Mixing the Syrup (or Butter) Through Your Popped Corn," in Chapter 3.
4. Heat in a 200° oven while fixing other ingredients

   • 2½ quarts (10 cups) popped corn

5. Measure into a heavy pan (such as a cast-iron pressure cooker)

- ½ cup sugar
- ½ cup brown sugar, firmly packed
- ¼ cup light corn syrup
- ¼ cup water

6. Cook to firm ball stage, stirring occasionally.

7. Remove from heat and add

- 1 tablespoon butter

8. Pour syrup over popped corn and mix well.

9. Fill a large bowl with water in which to rinse your hands as you work.

10. Form popcorn into tiny, bite-sized balls.

11. Insert wooden fondue picks into balls and arrange on serving platter.

12. Invite guests to dip corn balls into chocolate fondue; recipe follows.

The Chocolate Fondue

Don't worry if this recipe turns stiff after it has been stored in the refrigerator. Just add more cream or milk and beat again with a hand or electric mixer. If you have any left over from your fondue party, reheat it in a double boiler to serve over vanilla ice cream for a delicious hot fudge sundae.

1. Put water in bottom half of double boiler and set on stove over medium low heat.

2. Place in top of double boiler

- 2 cans sweetened condensed milk
- 3 ozs. (3 squares) unsweetened baking
  chocolate

29

3. Cook in double boiler 1 hour.

4. Check water in bottom of double boiler at 15-minute intervals and refill if necessary.

5. Remove fondue from heat and add

- ¼ cup light cream or homogenized milk (more if desired)

6. Beat with electric or hand mixer until smooth.

7. Pour chocolate fondue into fondue pot and reheat over very low heat to serve with corn balls.

Yield: 75 tiny balls (8–10 people)

Popcorn String Bird Feeder

This is certain to please the hungry birds in January.

Non-food items you will need: nylon cord or dental floss, needle.

1. Set aside

    • 2 cups popped corn

2. Cut into small pieces

    • 2 lbs. suet

3. Thread a needle with nylon cord or dental floss.
4. String alternately the suet and popcorn.
5. Hang from porch or eaves, as far as possible from fruit trees (especially cherry trees) that birds molest in the summer.

FEBRUARY

Groundhog Day

TANGY LEMON POPCORN

According to legend, we will have six more weeks of winter if the groundhog sees his shadow on February 2. But you'll feel sunny—no matter what the weather is like outside—with a bowlful of tangy lemon popcorn to munch on.

Non-food items you will need: two long-handled spoons, roasting pan, heavy pan, waxed paper.

1. Read "Testing the Syrup for Sugared Popcorn Recipes," in Chapter 3.
2. Read "Mixing the Syrup (or Butter) Through Your Popped Corn," in Chapter 3.
3. Heat in a 200° oven while fixing other ingredients

* 5 quarts (20 cups) popped corn

4. Measure into a heavy pan (such as a cast-iron pressure cooker)
* 2 cups sugar
* 1 6-oz. can (¾ cup) frozen lemonade concentrate
* ¾ cup water
* grated rind of 1 lemon
* ½ cup light corn syrup
* 1 teaspoon vinegar
* ¼ teaspoon salt

5. Cook over medium high heat to firm ball stage, stirring frequently.

6. Pour syrup over popped corn and mix well.
7. Set candied popcorn on waxed paper to harden.
8. Break into chunks when cool.

Yield: 15 servings

Lincoln's Birthday

POPCORN LOG CABIN CENTERPIECE

In honor of Abe Lincoln's birthday or another February event, you may want to make a popcorn "log" cabin center-piece.

The non-stick coating called for in this and other recipes comes in a spray can and may be purchased in the cooking oil section of your grocery store. It is less messy and less likely to add a foreign taste to your popcorn than will regular cooking oil, but you may substitute the oil if you prefer.

Non-food items you will need: two long-handled spoons, roasting pan, heavy cardboard, ruler, pencil, scissors, scotch or masking tape, aluminum foil, non-stick coating, cooky sheet, heavy pan, large bowl.

Base for Log Cabin
Line a cardboard box 9½ inches long by 7½ inches wide and 4 inches deep with aluminum foil, or make a cardboard form for the base of the cabin according to the directions below:

1. Cut from heavy cardboard two strips measuring 9½ inches by 4 inches.
2. Cut from heavy cardboard two strips measuring 7½ inches by 4 inches.
3. With masking tape (or clear tape) fasten the shorter pieces between the longer ones into one long strip measuring 34 inches by 4 inches. Leave slight cracks between the strips as you tape them to allow for folding.

36

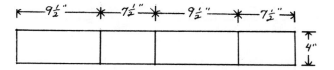

4. Line the entire strip with aluminum foil. Tape the foil to the cardboard in a few places to prevent slipping.
5. Spray the foil with non-stick coating.
6. Tape the two ends of the long strip together, folding at the cracks to form a rectangle. (Aluminum foil inside.)

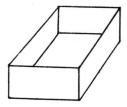

7. Place the rectangle, hollow side down, on a cooky sheet covered with aluminum foil and sprayed with non-stick coating.
8. Fill with candied popcorn according to directions on p. 38.

Roof for Log Cabin

1. Cut from heavy cardboard two pieces measuring 10½ inches by 7 inches.
2. Cut from heavy cardboard one piece measuring 10½ inches by 8½ inches.
3. Tape the three pieces together on the 10½-inch sides into one long piece of cardboard measuring 22½ inches by 10½ inches. Leave slight cracks between the strips as you tape them to allow for folding.

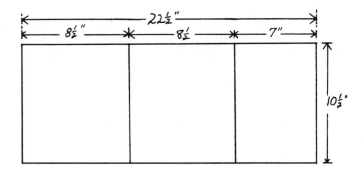

4. Line the entire piece of cardboard with aluminum foil. Tape the foil to the cardboard in a few places to prevent slipping.

5. Spray the foil with non-stick coating.

6. Tape the two outside edges together, folding at the cracks to form a triangle. (Aluminum foil inside.)

7. Place the triangle, hollow side down, on a cooky sheet covered with aluminum foil and sprayed with non-stick coating.

8. Fill with candied popcorn according to directions on p. 38.

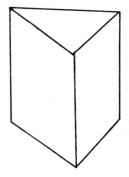

Candied Popcorn for Log Cabin

You will have to make this recipe twice, once for the base of the cabin and once for the roof. Do not try to double the recipe, however, because you will have trouble mixing it all at once.

38

1. Read "Testing the Syrup for Sugared Popcorn Recipes," in Chapter 3.

2. Read "Mixing the Syrup (or Butter) Through Your Popped Corn," in Chapter 3.

3. Heat in a 200° oven while fixing other ingredients

- 5 quarts (20 cups) popped corn

4. Measure into heavy pan (such as a cast-iron pressure cooker)

- 1 cup sugar
- ½ cup brown sugar, firmly packed
- ½ cup dark corn syrup
- ½ cup water

5. Cook to firm ball stage, stirring constantly.

6. Remove from heat and add

- 1 tablespoon butter

7. Pour syrup over popped corn and mix well.

8. Fill a large bowl with water in which to rinse your hands as you work.

9. Pack the candied popcorn into the cardboard form for the base of the log cabin, paying particular attention to filling the corners well. The recipe will not quite fill the container, but you should have some extra popcorn from the next batch.

10. Wash your utensils.

11. Make a second batch of candied popcorn, following the instructions above.

12. Pack the candied popcorn into the cardboard form for the roof of the log cabin, paying particular attention to filling the corners well. This recipe will more than fill the cardboard form for the roof. With the extra popcorn shape a small rectangular chimney to put on the roof. Use any remaining popcorn to fill the empty space in the form for the base of the log cabin.

Putting Up the Building

1. Let base, roof, and chimney of log cabin harden for ½ hour.

2. Remove tape from a corner of each form to expose base and roof of log cabin.

3. Set roof on base, largest side down.

4. Stick chimney on roof, shaping bottom to fit properly.

5. Wipe aluminum foil with clean, damp cloth and save it for re-use.

6. Store cardboard forms for re-use. (St. Patrick's Day castle and Christmas house call for same forms.)

7. Make doors and windows, if desired, with icing and cake decorator. Doors may also be made from lengths of stick licorice, arranged side by side, like a log door.

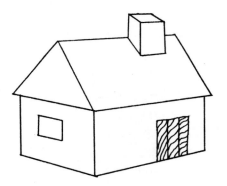

Valentine's Day

The following popcorn treats are three delicious ways to say "I love you" to the special people in your life on Valentine's Day.

CINNAMON POPCORN HEARTS

The cinnamon oil listed as an optional ingredient for this recipe may be purchased from a pharmacy, rather than a grocery store. *Be careful not to spill it on your skin or to rub it in your eyes.* Do not use it except near a supply of clean water so that you can wash your skin or eyes immediately in case of accident.

Non-food items you will need: two long-handled spoons, roasting pan, heavy pan, heart-shaped cooky cutters or gelatin molds, non-stick coating, plastic wrap or cellophane, ribbon, waxed paper.

1. Read "Testing the Syrup for Sugared Popcorn Recipes," in Chapter 3.
2. Read "Mixing the Syrup (or Butter) Through Your Popped Corn," in Chapter 3.
3. Heat in a 200° oven while fixing other ingredients

> • 5 quarts (20 cups) popped corn

4. Measure into a heavy pan (such as a cast-iron pressure cooker)

> • 1½ cups sugar
> • 1½ cups water

- ¼ teaspoon salt
- 1 cup red cinnamon candies
- ¼ teaspoon cinnamon oil (optional)
- ½ cup light corn syrup
- 1 teaspoon vinegar
- ¼ teaspoon red food coloring

5. Cook over medium heat, stirring until cinnamon candies are dissolved, to firm ball stage.

6. Pour syrup over popped corn and mix well.

7. Spray heart-shaped cooky cutters or gelatin molds with non-stick coating.

8. Press candied popcorn into molds and let harden for 2–3 minutes.

9. Remove gently with a sharp knife and set on waxed paper until firm.

10. While popcorn is still warm, place a colored valentine candy on top of each heart, if desired.

11. Wrap in plastic wrap or cellophane and tie with a red bow.

Yield: 24–30 medium-sized hearts

GUMDROP NOSEGAYS

Many butchers will give or sell you wooden skewers the right size for popcorn nosegays and suckers. Handicraft supply stores sell flat popsicle sticks which work equally well and which cost less than 1 cent apiece. You can also buy dowels at lumber stores and saw them into 5-inch lengths, but these will be less convenient and may also cost you more money.

Non-food items you will need: two long-handled spoons, roasting pan, heavy pan, large bowl, wooden skewers or popsicle sticks, 4-inch paper doilies, ¼-inch pink satin ribbon, plastic wrap or clear cellophane, scissors.

1. Read "Testing the Syrup for Sugared Popcorn Recipes," in Chapter 3.
2. Read "Mixing the Syrup (or Butter) Through Your Popped Corn," in Chapter 3.
3. Set aside

- 10 wooden skewers
- 10 small paper doilies
- 7 yards ¼-inch-wide pink satin ribbon

4. Cut into halves and set aside

- 2 cups small gumdrops

5. Heat in a 200° oven while fixing remaining ingredients

- 3 quarts (12 cups) popped corn

6. Measure into a heavy pan (such as a cast-iron pressure cooker)

- 1 cup sugar
- ½ cup light corn syrup
- ⅓ cup water

43

- ¼ cup (½ stick) butter
- ½ teaspoon salt

7. Cook over medium heat, stirring occasionally, to firm ball stage.

8. Remove from heat and stir in

- 1 teaspoon vanilla

9. Add gumdrops to popped corn.

10. Pour syrup over popped corn and mix well.

11. Fill a large bowl with water in which to rinse your hands as you work.

12. Mold popcorn into 10 balls and stick a wooden skewer in each.

13. Wrap balls in clear cellophane or plastic wrap.

14. Slit centers of paper doilies with scissors and poke skewers through them.

15. Cut ribbon into 25-inch lengths.

16. Tie a bow with long streamers around each skewer under the doily.

STRAWBERRY VALENTINE PIE

This holiday dessert looks beautiful and tastes even better.

Non-food items you will need: two long-handled spoons, roasting pan, heavy pan, two large bowls, 9-inch cake or pie tin, teakettle, small bowl, electric mixer.

The Popcorn Crust

1. Read "Testing the Syrup for Sugared Popcorn Recipes," in Chapter 3.

2. Read "Mixing the Syrup (or Butter) Through Your Popped Corn," in Chapter 3.

3. Heat in a 200° oven while fixing other ingredients

- 2 quarts (8 cups) popped corn

4. Measure into a heavy pan (such as a cast-iron pressure cooker)

- ¾ cup sugar
- ¼ cup light corn syrup
- ¼ cup water
- 1 tablespoon butter

5. Cook over medium heat to firm ball stage, stirring constantly.

6. Pour syrup over popped corn and mix well.

7. Fill a large bowl with water in which to rinse your hands while you work.

8. Press candied popcorn into 9-inch pie or cake tin, building edges higher than those of the tin.

9. Fill with strawberry cream filling; recipe follows.

The Strawberry Cream Filling

1. Set aside for later use

- ¾ cup miniature marshmallows

45

2. Fill teakettle with water and put on stove to boil.

3. Empty into large bowl

- 1 package strawberry gelatin

4. Pour over gelatin and stir until dissolved

- 1 cup boiling water

5. Beat until fluffy in small bowl with electric mixer

- 1 cup whipping cream (or 2 envelopes dry non-dairy topping, mixed according to directions). Set aside.

6. Add to gelatin

- 1 tray ice cubes

7. Stir gelatin and ice cubes until gelatin becomes very thick and starts to set. Remove remaining ice cubes and throw away.

8. Fold into gelatin with a spoon

- whipped cream
- 1 10-oz. package frozen strawberries broken with a fork.

9. Spoon gelatin mixture into popcorn crust.

10. Decorate top of pie with miniature marshmallows set in shape of a heart.

11. Put pie in refrigerator for 2 hours.

Washington's Birthday

CHERRY POPCORN BALLS

George Washington really didn't chop down that cherry tree, but he probably would have enjoyed these great-tasting cherry popcorn balls.

Non-food items you will need: two long-handled spoons, roasting pan, double boiler, large bowl.

1. Read "Mixing the Syrup (or Butter) Through Your Popped Corn," in Chapter 3.
2. Heat in a 200° oven while fixing other ingredients

- 2 quarts (8 cups) popped corn

3. Chop into small pieces and set on a paper towel to drain

- ½ cup maraschino cherries

4. Put water in bottom of double boiler and place on medium high heat.
5. Measure into top of double boiler

- 4 cups (approximately ½ lb.) miniature marshmallows
- ¼ cup (½ stick) butter

6. Place top of double boiler over bottom and stir marshmallows until dissolved.
7. Mix cherries with popped corn.
8. Pour marshmallow mixture over popped corn and mix well.

9. Fill a large bowl with water in which to rinse your hands as you work.

10. Shape popcorn into balls.

Yield: 6 balls

February Birthday Treat

PINK CLOWN POPCONES

These smiley clown faces will put smiles on the faces of your birthday guests. And you'll have fun making them, too.

Non-food items you will need: two long-handled spoons, roasting pan, heavy pan, large bowl, scissors, waxed paper.

1. Read "Testing the Syrup for Sugared Popcorn Recipes," in Chapter 3.
2. Read "Mixing the Syrup (or Butter) Through Your Popped Corn," in Chapter 3.
3. Set aside for later use

- 10 ice cream cones (pointed ends)
- ¾ cup colored gumdrops

4. Heat in a 200° oven while fixing other ingredients

- 5 quarts (20 cups) popped corn

5. Measure into a heavy pan (such as a cast-iron pressure cooker)
- 2 cups sugar
- ⅔ cup light cream (or evaporated milk)
- 2 tablespoons light corn syrup
- 4 drops red food coloring

6. Cook to soft ball stage over medium low heat, stirring constantly. (Do not stop stirring for an instant, even while you test the syrup in cold water, because this recipe burns very easily.)

7. Remove from heat and stir in

- 1 tablespoon butter
- 1 teaspoon imitation strawberry or raspberry flavoring

8. Pour the syrup over the popped corn and mix well.

9. Fill a large bowl with water in which to rinse your hands as you work.

10. Fill the cones with candied popcorn, rounding the tops like huge scoops of ice cream. Make the "scoops" as even as possible since they will be the heads for your clowns.

11. Turn the cones upside down and set on waxed paper. Tip the point of each cone like a jaunty clown hat and flatten the "scoop" of popcorn so the clown head won't roll.

12. Give each clown a pompon on the tip of his hat with a colored gumdrop. Use whole red gumdrops for noses and cut the remaining gumdrops with scissors for eyes and mouths.

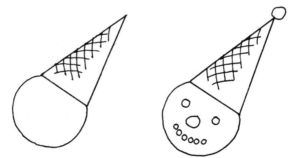

Yield: 10 clowns (cones lightly packed and small heads) or 8 clowns with larger heads

MARCH

St. Patrick's Day

GREEN CASTLE CENTERPIECE

Ireland is full of interesting old castles, so St. Patrick's Day seems like an appropriate time to make one of popcorn— green popcorn, of course!

Non-food items you will need: two long-handled spoons, roasting pan, heavy cardboard, ruler, pencil, scissors, scotch or masking tape, aluminum foil, non-stick coating, cooky sheet, heavy pan, large bowl, dowels, colored wrapping paper, toothpicks, glue, double boiler.

Base for Castle
1. Follow the same instructions as for the log cabin base, p. 36.
Candied Popcorn for Castle Base
1. Read "Testing the Syrup for Sugared Popcorn Recipes," in Chapter 3.
2. Read "Mixing the Syrup (or Butter) Through Your Popped Corn," in Chapter 3.
3. Heat in a 200° oven while fixing other ingredients

- 6 quarts (24 cups) popped corn

4. Measure into a heavy pan (such as a cast-iron pressure cooker)

- ¾ cup sugar
- 1½ cups light corn syrup
- 1½ packages undissolved lime gelatin
- 6 drops green food coloring

5. Cook over medium heat, stirring constantly, until mixture boils vigorously.

6. Remove syrup from stove and pour over popped corn. Mix well.

7. Fill a large bowl with water in which to rinse your hands as you work.

8. Pack the candied popcorn into the cardboard form for the base of the castle, paying particular attention to filling the corners well.

9. Wash cooking utensils to make another batch of the same recipe for the towers of the castle.

Towers for Castle

1. Set aside

- 4 wooden dowels 10 to 12 inches long
- 5 wooden dowels 5 to 7 inches long

Candied Popcorn for Castle Towers

1. Make a second batch of green popcorn from recipe above ("Candied Popcorn for Castle Base").

Making the Towers

1. Fill a large bowl with water in which to rinse your hands as you work.

2. Mold the popcorn around the 9 short and long dowels into cylinders which are flat on both ends. Do not worry about getting your towers exactly the same size because medieval castles were never symmetrical.

3. Allow towers to harden at least ½ hour.

Assembling the Castle

1. Set aside

- 5–6 pointed ice cream cones

- 5–6 sturdy toothpicks
- colored wrapping paper
- gumdrops
- licorice twists
- cardboard
- scissors
- white glue
- assorted candies

2. For each flag cut two triangles or two rectangles exactly the same size from colored wrapping paper.

3. Glue the two sides of the flags together with toothpicks between them, as shown.

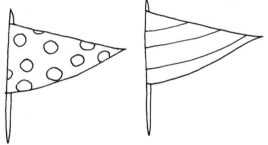

4. Cut rectangles from heavy cardboard the right size for door and drawbridge.

5. Cut licorice twists the same lengths as door and drawbridge.

6. Attach licorice twists, side by side, on cardboard rectangles with regular glue. (These will be inedible, since they will be permanently stuck to the cardboard.)

7. Remove tape from one corner of the form to expose the base of the castle.

8. Make "glue" for assembling the remainder of the castle by melting in the top of a double boiler

- 1 cup miniature marshmallows
- 2 teaspoons butter

9. Stir "glue" well.

10. Stick the 4 long towers upright next to the 4 corners of the base with marshmallow "glue." Stick the 5 short towers upright on top of the base.

11. Attach the door to one end of the castle.

12. Decorate castle with inverted ice cream cones on 5 or 6 of the towers. Stick flags in the cones.

13. Line the top outside edge of the castle with gumdrops.

14. Attach assorted candies to castle for windows.

15. Add drawbridge as shown.

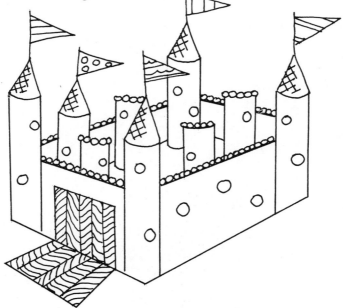

16. Wipe aluminum foil from the form with a clean, damp cloth and save it for re-use.

17. Store cardboard form for re-use.

GREEN POPCORN SHAMROCKS

These popcorn treats will bring the luck of the Irish to any-
one.

Non-food items you will need: two long-handled spoons,
roasting pan, heavy pan, shamrock cooky cutters, non-stick
coating, large bowl, waxed paper.

For the shamrock form use a "club"-shaped cooky cutter
from a set of playing card cooky cutters.

1. Read "Testing the Syrup for Sugared Popcorn Recipes,"
in Chapter 3.
2. Read "Mixing the Syrup (or Butter) Through Your
Popped Corn," in Chapter 3.
3. Heat in a 200° oven while fixing other ingredients

- 5 quarts (20 cups) popped corn

4. Measure into a heavy pan (such as a cast-iron pressure
cooker)

- 1½ cups sugar
- ½ cup light corn syrup
- ½ cup water
- ½ teaspoon green food coloring

5. Cook to firm ball stage over medium high heat, stirring
frequently.
6. Remove from stove and add

- 1 tablespoon butter
- 1 teaspoon wintergreen or mint flavoring

7. Pour syrup over popped corn and mix well.
8. Spray a shamrock cooky cutter with non-stick coating.

9. Fill a large bowl with water in which to rinse your hands as you work.

10. Press the candied popcorn into the cooky cutter. Allow to harden for 2–3 minutes. Loosen the popcorn carefully with a sharp knife and set on waxed paper until firm.

11. Refill the cooky cutter with popcorn, spraying the cutter with non-stick coating when necessary.

Yield: 30 very small shamrocks

March Birthday Treat

PINK POPCORN MINT CAKE

This birthday cake is as delicious as it is different. It may or may not be served with ice cream.

Non-food items you will need: two long-handled spoons, roasting pan, angel food cake pan, aluminum foil, non-stick coating, heavy plastic bag, rolling pin, double boiler.

1. Read "Mixing the Syrup (or Butter) Through Your Popped Corn," in Chapter 3.
2. Line an angel food cake pan with aluminum foil and spray with non-stick coating.
3. Heat in a 200° oven while fixing other ingredients

- 6 quarts (24 cups) popped corn

4. Put in a heavy plastic bag and roll with a rolling pin to crush

- 1 lb. pink peppermint candy

5. Put water in bottom of a double boiler and set on the stove to boil.
6. Put in the top of double boiler

- 2 lbs. miniature mashmallows
- ½ cup (1 stick) butter

7. If pan is overcrowded, separate ingredients into halves and prepare as two batches.

59

8. Stir marshmallows and butter over boiling water in double boiler until completely melted.

9. Add crushed peppermint candy.

10. Pour mixture over popped corn and mix well.

11. Pack popcorn into angel food cake pan.

12. Cool for ½ hour and remove from pan by gently lifting foil and then peeling it away.

13. If desired, frost the top only with chocolate icing, or dribble melted dipping chocolate on the top and down the sides.

14. Serve with ice cream, if you prefer.

APRIL

April Fools' Day

CRAZY CHOCOLATE POPCORN BALLS

Here's an April Fools' joke your friends will like.

Non-food items you will need: two long-handled spoons, roasting pan, small plastic medicine bottles, jokebook, paper, pen or pencil, scissors, heavy pan.

1. Ask your druggist to give or sell you 12 empty plastic medicine bottles (smallest size).
2. Copy 12 jokes from a jokebook and put them in the bottles. Put lids on the bottles.
3. Read "Testing the Syrup for Sugared Popcorn Recipes," in Chapter 3.
4. Read "Mixing the Syrup (or Butter) Through Your Popped Corn," in Chapter 3.
5. Heat in a 200° oven while fixing other ingredients

  • 3 quarts (12 cups) popped corn

6. Measure into a heavy pan (such as a cast-iron pressure cooker)
  • 2 cups sugar
  • ½ cup light corn syrup
  • 1 cup water
  • 2 ozs. (2 squares) unsweetened chocolate

7. Cook over medium heat to soft ball stage, stirring frequently.
8. Pour syrup over popped corn and mix well.
9. Form into balls around plastic medicine bottles.

Yield: 12 balls

Easter

POPCORN EASTER BASKET

You can eat these eggs—and the basket, too!

Non-food items you will need: two long-handled spoons, roasting pan, heavy pan, 3-quart mixing bowl, aluminum foil, non-stick coating, large bowl, heavy wire, wire clippers.

Candied Popcorn for Easter Basket
1. Read "Testing the Syrup for Sugared Popcorn Recipes," in Chapter 3.
2. Read "Mixing the Syrup (or Butter) Through Your Popped Corn," in Chapter 3.
3. Heat in a 200° oven while fixing other ingredients

   • 4½ quarts (18 cups) popped corn

4. Measure into a heavy pan (such as a cast-iron pressure cooker)
   • 2 cups sugar
   • ¾ cup dark corn syrup
   • ¾ cup water
   • ¼ teaspoon salt

5. Cook over medium high heat to firm ball stage, stirring occasionally.
6. Pour syrup over popped corn and mix well.

Making the Basket
1. Line a 3-quart mixing bowl with aluminum foil and spray with non-stick coating.

2. Fill a large bowl with water in which to rinse your hands as you work.

3. Pat a layer of candied popcorn inside the bowl on the aluminum foil.

4. Allow popcorn to harden 4–5 minutes.

5. Form a sturdy wire into a half circle approximately the same size as the bowl would be if turned upside down.

6. Stick the ends of the wire into opposite sides of the popcorn basket.

7. Make a handle for the basket by pressing extra popcorn from recipe along the wire. Be sure that the popcorn of the handle (not merely the wire) is fastened securely to the popcorn sides of the basket.

8. Let basket harden overnight.

9. Fill with lightweight Easter candies, such as marshmallow bunnies, and popcorn Easter eggs; recipe follows.

Candied Popcorn for Easter Eggs

1. Select several different flavors and colors of fruit gelatin to make three or more batches of the following recipe.

2. Read "Mixing the Syrup (or Butter) Through Your Popped Corn," in Chapter 3.

3. Heat in a 200° oven while fixing other ingredients

- 4 quarts (16 cups) popped corn

4. Measure into a heavy pan (such as a cast-iron pressure cooker)

- ½ cup sugar
- 1 cup light corn syrup
- 1 package undissolved fruit-flavored gelatin
- 4 drops food coloring (same color as gelatin)

5. Cook over medium heat, stirring constantly, until mixture boils vigorously.

6. Pour syrup over popped corn and mix well.

7. Fill a large bowl with water in which to rinse your hands as you work.

8. Form popcorn into egg-shaped balls.

Yield: 16–20 popcorn eggs

April Birthday Centerpiece

POPCORN TREE

These popcorn blossoms will bring springtime beauty to your dining room table.

Non-food items you will need: two long-handled spoons, roasting pan, branch from bush or tree, wooden block, drill, double boiler, large bowl, paper parasols (optional), waxed paper.

The Stand
1. Prune a graceful, full branch about 10 or 12 inches long from a tree or bush.
2. Drill a hole in a sturdy block of wood and insert the branch upright to resemble a growing tree.

Candied Popcorn for the Tree
1. Read "Mixing the Syrup (or Butter) Through Your Popped Corn," in Chapter 3.
2. Heat in a 200° oven while fixing other ingredients

  • 3 quarts (12 cups) popped corn

3. Put water in bottom half of a double boiler and place on stove to heat.
4. Measure into top of double boiler

  • 1 lb. miniature marshmallows
  • ¼ cup (½ stick) butter
  • 3 tablespoons undissolved peach gelatin or
    3 drops orange food coloring

66

5. Set top of double boiler over boiling water and stir marsh-mallows vigorously until thoroughly dissolved and blended with gelatin.

6. Pour syrup over popped corn and mix well.

Assembling the Tree

1. Fill a large bowl with water in which to rinse your hands as you work.

2. Attach clusters of candied popcorn along the shoots of the branch to resemble an apricot tree in bloom.

3. Place any extra candied popcorn on waxed paper and allow it to harden.

4. When tree is fully dry, decorate it further with miniature paper parasols (some open and some closed) among the popcorn apricot blossoms.

5. Break the extra popcorn into small chunks and put it inside a paper parasol for each guest.

6. Save your popcorn tree in a large plastic bag for future parties. Other ideas you can try instead of the paper parasols are these:

    a. Kites cut from colored construction paper (yarn tails).

    b. Tiny favors for guests such as whistles, sticks of gum, dolls, etc. tied to the tree with ribbons.

MAY

Mother's Day

MOTHER'S DAY TABLE DECORATIONS

These attractive popcorn flowerpots with fabric flowers can be placed individually by each table setting as favors and also arranged in the center of the table as a centerpiece. They are made in two stages—first the fabric flowers and then the popcorn flowerpots.

Non-food items you will need: two long-handled spoons, roasting pan, scissors, white glue, scraps of print fabrics, small yellow pompons, green pipe cleaners, small round medicine bottle, heavy pan, muffin tins, non-stick coating, waxed paper.

Fabric Flowers for Table Decorations

1. Assemble on a working table

- scissors
- white glue
- scraps of gay cotton print fabrics
- small yellow pompons (one for each flower)
- green pipe cleaners (at least 6 pieces for each flower, about 5–8 inches long)
- empty round medicine bottle, about 1½ inches in diameter

2. Working from one end of a piece of pipe cleaner, wrap it around the medicine bottle to shape a circle with a tail.
3. Slip pipe cleaner off bottle and twist to hold shape.
4. Put glue around the circle (not the tail) of the pipe cleaner and stick to the RIGHT side of a piece of fabric.

70

5. Allow to dry.

6. With scissors, cut the fabric in a circle on the outside edge of the pipe cleaner. You now have 1 petal for your flower.

7. You will need 4 more petals for your flower (plus 1 or 2 leaves, if you would like them, too), so repeat steps 2, 3, 4, 5, and 6.

8. Twist the five tails of the pipe cleaners together, and attach them to one longer piece of pipe cleaner.

9. Cut away extra pipe cleaner from tails.

10. Paste a pompon in the center where petals are joined. You now have a fabric flower with five petals.

11. Make as many flowers as there are people in your family plus a few extra ones to set in a bunch in the middle of the table.

Popcorn Flowerpots for Fabric Flowers

1. Read "Testing the Syrup for Sugared Popcorn Recipes," in Chapter 3.

2. Read "Mixing the Syrup (or Butter) Through Your Popped Corn," in Chapter 3.

3. Heat in a 200° oven while fixing other ingredients

- 3 quarts (12 cups) popped corn

4. Measure into a heavy pan (such as a cast-iron pressure cooker)

- ½ cup dark brown corn syrup
- ½ cup sugar
- ½ cup brown sugar, firmly packed
- ¼ cup water
- ¼ cup (½ stick) butter
- 2 teaspoons vinegar
- ¼ teaspoon salt

5. Cook to firm ball stage, stirring occasionally.

6. Pour syrup over popped corn and mix well.

7. Spray muffin tins with non-stick coating.

8. Working quickly so popcorn won't harden before it is molded, press it firmly into muffin tins.

9. Let popcorn harden for 3–4 minutes.

10. Remove popcorn gently with a sharp knife and set on waxed paper (small side down) to dry.

11. Put a fabric flower in the center of each flowerpot.

Yield: 17 flowerpots

PINEAPPLE POPCORN ICE CREAM SUNDAES

The unusual blend of flavors in this dessert makes a special event like Mother's Day seem even more festive. But if your mom is trying to lose weight, skip this recipe and go on to the next one.

Non-food items you will need: two long-handled spoons, roasting pan, heavy pan, individual doughnut-shaped gelatin molds, non-stick coating.

1. Read "Mixing the Syrup (or Butter) Through Your Popped Corn," in Chapter 3.

2. Heat in a 200° oven while fixing the other ingredients

- 1½ quarts (6 cups) popped corn

3. Measure into a heavy pan (such as a cast-iron pressure cooker)

- ½ cup (1 stick) butter
- 1½ cups light brown sugar, firmly packed
- ¼ teaspoon salt

4. Heat over low heat, stirring constantly, until sugar melts and mixture bubbles.

5. Pour mixture over popcorn and mix well.

6. Spray 8 doughnut-shaped gelatin molds with non-stick coating.

7. Press popcorn into molds and let harden.

8. Remove popcorn shells gently with sharp knife and place on individual serving dishes to cool.

9. Place on each shell

- one scoop of vanilla ice cream

10. Top with

- unsweetened crushed pineapple

Yield: 8 servings

LO-CAL POPCORN

Popcorn would be much better for us if we could learn to eat it as the Indians did—without either sugar or butter. This recipe is almost as non-fattening but somewhat tastier than unflavored popcorn. It might not knock you off your feet at first, but for your health's sake it is worth acquiring a taste for.

Non-food items you will need: two long-handled spoons, roasting pan.

1. Read "Mixing the Syrup (or Butter) Through Your Popped Corn," in Chapter 3.

2. Place in a large pan (such as a roasting pan)

   • 3 quarts (12 cups) popped corn

3. Shake well before measuring

   • ¼ cup low-calorie salad dressing (your favorite brand)

4. Pour salad dressing over corn and mix well.

Yield: 10–12 servings

May Birthday Centerpiece

BUTTER RUM POPCORN

This popcorn is as tasty as the rum that pirates used to drink and as brilliant as the gold they sought. Put some inside a miniature treasure chest as a centerpiece for a May birthday, treasure hunt party, or any other special occasion.

Non-food items you will need: two long-handled spoons, roasting pan, heavy pan, pirate chest, waxed paper.

1. Read "Testing the Syrup for Sugared Popcorn Recipes," in Chapter 3.
2. Read "Mixing the Syrup (or Butter) Through Your Popped Corn," in Chapter 3.
3. Heat in a 200° oven while fixing other ingredients

- 4 quarts (16 cups) popped corn

4. Measure into a heavy pan (such as a cast-iron pressure cooker)
- ½ cup sugar
- ⅔ cup light corn syrup
- ⅓ cup water
- 2 teaspoons vinegar
- ¼ teaspoon salt
- ¼ teaspoon orange food coloring

5. Cook over medium high heat to soft ball stage, stirring occasionally.
6. Remove from heat and add

- ¼ cup (½ stick) butter
- 1 teaspoon imitation rum flavoring

7. Pour syrup over popped corn and mix well.
8. Set popcorn on waxed paper to cool.
9. Break in chunks and place in pirate chest.

Yield: "pirate's gold" for 10–12 buccaneers

JUNE

Flag Day

CHOCOLATE POPPERS

These unusual popcorn treats look like cookies and taste like fudge.

Non-food items you will need: two long-handled spoons, roasting pan, heavy pan, waxed paper.

1. Read "Mixing the Syrup (or Butter) Through Your Popped Corn," in Chapter 3, but *do not* place corn in oven to pre-heat.

2. Combine in large roasting pan

- 2 cups popped corn
- 1 cup miniature marshmallows

3. Measure into a heavy pan (such as a cast-iron pressure cooker)

- ¾ cup sugar
- ½ cup evaporated milk
- 2 tablespoons butter

4. Bring to a full boil and cook three more minutes, stirring constantly.

5. Remove from heat and add

- 1 cup semi-sweet chocolate pieces

6. Stir until smooth.

7. Cool approximately 15 minutes.

8. Pour fudge mixture over popped corn and mix well.

9. Drop by teaspoons onto waxed paper and cool until firm.

Yield: 30 small poppers

Graduation Day

POPCORN-NUT MACAROONS

A gift you make in your kitchen expresses your love and consideration better than something you can buy. Here is a possible present for a June graduate.

Non-food items you will need: nut chopper, large and small bowls, hand or electric mixer, cooky sheet, cake rack.

1. Set oven to 250°.

2. Put through a nut chopper and then measure

- 1 cup popped corn

3. Put popcorn in a large bowl and add

- 1 cup coarsely chopped pecans or walnuts

4. Place in a small bowl and beat with hand or electric mixer until it forms stiff peaks

- 1 egg white

5. Gradually add (1 teaspoon at a time) while beating

- ½ cup sugar

6. Continue beating and add

- ¼ teaspoon salt
- 1 teaspoon vanilla

7. Gently pour egg white mixture over dry mixture, stirring slowly by hand.

8. Grease a cooky sheet.

81

9. Drop popcorn mixture onto cooky sheet by heaping tea-spoons.

10. Bake for 20 minutes.

11. Cool slightly and then remove from cooky sheet onto cake rack.

Yield: 30 small macaroons

Father's Day

SUPER SENSATIONAL
CARAMEL POPCORN BALLS

This recipe is also super fattening and super difficult. Oh
well. Father's Day comes only once a year.

Non-food items you will need: two long-handled spoons,
roasting pan, heavy pan, large bowl.

1. Read "Testing the Syrup for Sugared Popcorn Recipes,"
in Chapter 3.
2. Read "Mixing the Syrup (or Butter) Through Your
Popped Corn," in Chapter 3.
3. Heat in a 200° oven while fixing other ingredients

  • 6 quarts (24 cups) popped corn

4. Cut into 8 chunks and set aside

  • 1 cup (2 sticks) butter

5. Measure into a heavy pan (such as a cast-iron pressure
cooker)
  • 1 cup brown sugar, firmly packed
  • 1 cup sugar
  • 1 cup light corn syrup
  • 1 cup sweetened condensed milk

6. Place over medium low heat, stirring constantly, until
mixture bubbles.
7. Add one chunk butter. When it has thoroughly melted,
add another. Repeat process, stirring constantly.

8. Cook to firm ball stage. (Note: This recipe burns *very easily,* and you should not stop stirring for an instant, even to test your syrup. If for any reason the syrup should start to burn, pour it immediately through a strainer into a clean pan and continue cooking.)

9. Pour syrup over popped corn and mix well.

10. Fill a large bowl with water in which to rinse your hands as you work.

11. Form popcorn into balls.

Yield: 20 balls

BEEFY POPCORN ALTERNATE
FOR DIETING DADS

The caramel popcorn recipe is fancier, but if Dad is on a diet, he may appreciate this high-protein recipe more. (It's better for you, too!)

Non-food items you will need: two long-handled spoons, roasting pan, double boiler.

1. Read "Mixing the Syrup (or Butter) Through Your Popped Corn," in Chapter 3.
2. Heat in a 200° oven while fixing other ingredients

- 3 quarts (12 cups) popped corn

3. Put water in bottom half of double boiler and set on stove to boil.
4. In top of double boiler melt

- ½ cup (1 stick) butter

5. Add

- 1 small (2½ oz.) jar dried beef, chopped

6. Soften beef in melted butter for 5 minutes.
7. Remove from stove and pour butter mixture over popped corn. Mix well.

Yield: 12–14 servings

June Birthday Treat

POPCORN BALLOONS

The red food coloring and fruit punch provide the basic color for these old-fashioned balloons, but the rest of the decoration is up to you.

Non-food items you will need: two long-handled spoons, roasting pan, heavy pan, large bowl, plastic wrap, nut cups, scissors, glue, sewing trims such as rickrack and ribbon.

Candied Popcorn for the Balloons
1. Read "Testing the Syrup for Sugared Popcorn Recipes," in Chapter 3.
2. Read "Mixing the Syrup (or Butter) Through Your Popped Corn," in Chapter 3.
3. Heat in a 200° oven while fixing other ingredients

- 5 quarts (20 cups) popped corn

4. Measure into a heavy pan (such as a cast-iron pressure cooker)

- 2 cups sugar
- 1 6-oz. can (¾ cup) frozen concentrate for red fruit punch
- ¾ cup water
- ½ cup light corn syrup
- 1 teaspoon vinegar
- 12 drops red food coloring
- ¼ teaspoon salt

5. Cook over medium high heat, stirring frequently, to soft ball stage.

6. Pour over popped corn and mix well.

7. Fill a large bowl with water in which to rinse your hands as you work.

8. Form into balls.

9. Wrap in plastic wrap.

Yield: 14 medium balls

Making the Balloons

1. Assemble on a working table

- 14 popcorn balloons wrapped in plastic
- 14 nut cups
- scissors
- glue
- sewing trims, such as rickrack, ribbon, etc.
- small candies, if desired

2. Decorate the nut cups with the sewing trims, making each one different. Glue trims in place on the cups.

3. Fill nut cups with small candies, if desired. Level of candy should not be above top of nut cup.

4. Place a popcorn ball on top of each nut cup to resemble a hydrogen balloon.

JULY

July 4th

POPCORN CANNONS

Salute America with cannons using candied popcorn both as the wheels and as the ammunition. They are made in three stages—the popcorn wheels, the cardboard cylinder, and the popcorn ammunition.

Non-food items you will need: two long-handled spoons, roasting pan, heavy pan, large bowl, 2½-inch biscuit cutter, non-stick coating, 11-inch cardboard tubes, popsicle sticks, scissors, clear tape aluminum foil or colored (red, white, and blue) wrapping paper, ruler, pencil, knife or saw, miniature flags, waxed paper.

The Popcorn Wheels
1. Read "Testing the Syrup for Sugared Popcorn Recipes," in Chapter 3.
2. Read "Mixing the Syrup (or Butter) Through Your Popped Corn," in Chapter 3.
3. Heat in a 200° oven while fixing other ingredients

· 2½ quarts (10 cups) popped corn

4. Measure into a heavy pan (such as a cast-iron pressure cooker)

· 1 cup sugar
· ¼ cup light corn syrup
· ¼ cup water
· 1 teaspoon vinegar
· 2 tablespoons butter

5. Cook to firm ball stage, stirring occasionally.

6. Pour syrup over popped corn and mix well.

7. Fill a large bowl with water in which to rinse your hands as you work.

8. Spray a 2½-inch biscuit cutter with non-stick coating.

9. Press popcorn into biscuit cutter and let harden for about 30 seconds.

10. Remove popcorn from biscuit cutter gently with a sharp knife and lay on waxed paper to harden.

Yield: 15 popcorn wheels

Making the Cannons

1. Assemble on a working table

- 11-inch-long cardboard tubes from inside rolls of paper towels, foil, plastic wrap, etc. (1 for each guest)
- popsicle sticks cut into 3-inch lengths (1 for each guest)
- scissors
- clear tape
- aluminum foil or red, white, and blue wrapping paper
- popcorn wheels

2. Cover one hollow end of each cardboard tube with two thicknesses of foil. Tape in place.

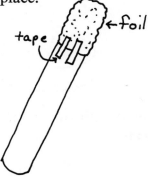

3. Leaving the free end open, cover the entire tube with foil or with red, white, and blue gift wrapping paper. Tape if necessary.

4. Insert a popcorn wheel on either end of a 3-inch popsicle stick.

5. With open ends up, rest the foil cannons on the popsicle sticks. Tape from underneath so cannons won't roll.

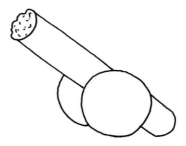

6. Stick miniature flags in extra popcorn wheels.

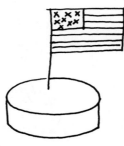

7. Fill cannons with sugared popcorn or brown sugar popcorn; recipes follow.

92

Sugared Popcorn for Ammunition
1. Read "Testing the Syrup for Sugared Popcorn Recipes," in Chapter 3.
2. Read "Mixing the Syrup (or Butter) Through Your Popped Corn," in Chapter 3.
3. Heat in a 200° oven while fixing other ingredients

· 6 quarts (24 cups) popped corn

4. Melt in a heavy pan (such as a cast-iron pressure cooker)

· 2 tablespoons butter
5. Add
· 2 cups sugar
· 1 cup water

6. Cook to firm ball stage, stirring frequently.
7. Remove from heat and add

· 1 teaspoon vanilla

8. Pour syrup over popped corn and mix well.
Note: This recipe is not suitable for balls or other popcorn shapes.

Brown Sugar Popcorn for Ammunition
1. Read "Testing the Syrup for Sugared Popcorn Recipes," in Chapter 3.
2. Read "Mixing the Syrup (or Butter) Through Your Popped Corn," in Chapter 3.
3. Heat in a 200° oven while fixing other ingredients

· 4 quarts (16 cups) popped corn

4. Melt in a heavy pan (such as a cast-iron pressure cooker)

· 2 tablespoons butter

5. Add

- 1½ cups brown sugar, firmly packed
- ⅓ cup water

6. Cook to soft ball stage, stirring frequently.

7. Remove from heat and add

- ½ teaspoon vanilla

8. Pour syrup over popped corn and mix well.

Note: This recipe is not suitable for balls or other popcorn shapes.

July Popcorn Picnic

ONION POPCORN

Dried onion added to buttered popcorn makes a zesty snack to take along on a picnic to the zoo, the park, or the tree house in your back yard. Take a thermos bottle full of milk to quench your thirst.

Non-food items you will need: 1-quart saucepan, two long-handled spoons, roasting pan, scissors.

1. Read "Mixing the Syrup (or Butter) Through Your Popped Corn," in Chapter 3.
2. Place in a large container (such as a roasting pan)

- 2 quarts (8 cups) popped corn

3. Measure

- 2 tablespoons dry onion soup mix

4. Snip onions into small pieces with scissors.
5. Melt in a saucepan over low heat

- ¼ cup (½ stick) butter

6. Add onion soup to melted butter and stir thoroughly.
7. Pour melted butter over popped corn and mix well.

Yield: enough for one hungry picnicker (several picnickers if they take oranges along, too)

July Birthday Treat

JIFFY CARAMEL LOLLIPOPCORN

These easy caramel lollipops taste even better when dipped in chocolate. (See recipe which follows.)

Non-food items you will need: two long-handled spoons, roasting pan, double boiler, large bowl, muffin tins, non-stick coating, wooden skewers or popsicle sticks, waxed paper.

1. Read "Mixing the Syrup (or Butter) Through Your Popped Corn," in Chapter 3.

2. Heat in a 200° oven while fixing other ingredients

> • 4 quarts (16 cups) popped corn

3. Put water in bottom half of double boiler and place on stove to boil.

4. Measure into top half of double boiler

> • 6 tablespoons water
> • 1 lb. (approximately 56) light caramels

5. Stir caramels until completely melted.

6. Pour syrup over popped corn and mix well.

7. Fill a large bowl with water in which to rinse your hands as you work.

8. Spray individual muffin tins with non-stick coating.

9. Press popcorn into muffin tins and let harden about 1 minute.

10. Stick skewer into each muffin tin full of popcorn.

11. Gently remove popcorn with a sharp knife and set on waxed paper to dry.

12. If desired, dip lollipops into chocolate after ½ hour or longer.

Yield: 22 small lollipops

Chocolate-Dipped Lollipops

1. Put water in bottom half of double boiler and place over high heat on stove. When water boils, turn temperature to simmer. Do not allow water to boil while melting chocolate.

2. In top of double boiler measure

- 1 tablespoon light corn syrup
- 2 lbs. dipping chocolate

3. Stir chocolate occasionally as it melts.

4. Dip the tops of each lollipop into the chocolate.

5. Set lollipops on waxed paper until chocolate is dry.

AUGUST

August Birthday Treat

POPCORN-FILLED CHUCK WAGONS

Give each cowpuncher at your Western party a popcorn-filled chuckwagon to take home. They are made in two steps —first the paper chuck wagons and then the popcorn filling. Most drugstores or stationery stores sell all the supplies you will need for the paper chuck wagons.

Non-food items you will need: two long-handled spoons, roasting pan, pencil, scissors, compass (or juice glass), ruler, sliding trays from boxes of wooden kitchen matches, brass paper fasteners, colored pipe cleaners, glue, colored wrapping paper or construction paper, cardboard, felt-tip pen, saucepan.

Making the Chuck Wagons
1. Assemble on a working table

- pencil
- scissors
- compass (or juice glass measuring 2 inches in diameter)
- ruler
- sliding trays from boxes of wooden kitchen matches (1 for each guest)
- brass paper fasteners (4 for each guest)
- colored pipe cleaners approximately 5 inches long (1 for each guest)
- glue
- colored gift wrapping paper or construction paper

100

- cardboard
- felt-tip pen

2. With pencil and compass (or juice glass) trace on cardboard 4 wheels for each wagon.

3. Cut out the wheels and draw spokes with felt-tip pen, if desired.

4. Attach wheels to match box with brass fasteners, extending them below bottom of box and beyond each end.

5. Poke pipe cleaner through center of one end of wagon.

6. Bend one end of pipe cleaner ¼ inch to prevent it from slipping back through hole. Bend other end to resemble a wagon handle.

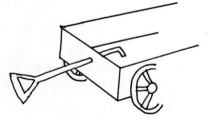

7. Measure and cut from colored construction paper a strip 4½″ x 8½″.

8. Put paper inside wagon to resemble the cover of a prairie schooner and glue in place.

9. Fill with bacon popcorn; recipe follows.

Bacon Popcorn

1. Read "Mixing the Syrup (or Butter) Through Your Popped Corn," in Chapter 3.

2. Measure into a large container (such as a roasting pan)

- 3 quarts (12 cups) popped corn

3. Melt in a saucepan over low heat

- ½ cup (1 stick) butter

4. Add

- ½ cup imitation bacon bits
- 1 teaspoon salt

5. Pour over popped corn and mix well.

Lemonade Stand Snack

BLUE CHEESE POPCORN

Keep your lemonade stand customers happy (and thirsty for more lemonade) by providing free salty or cheese-flavored popcorn. Here is one good recipe.

Non-food items you will need: 1-quart saucepan, two long-handled spoons, roasting pan.

1. Read "Mixing the Syrup (or Butter) Through Your Popped Corn," in Chapter 3.
2. Measure into a large pan (such as a roasting pan)

- 6 quarts (24 cups) popped corn

3. Melt in a saucepan over low heat

- 1 cup (2 sticks) butter

4. Remove from heat and stir in

- 1 package dry blue cheese salad dressing mix

5. Pour butter mixture over popped corn and mix well.

Yield: Enough popcorn to keep 8 customers thirsty.

SEPTEMBER

Labor Day

SPINACH AND POPCORN SALAD

Treat the breadwinners in your family to a hearty holiday meal including this unique salad.

Non-food items you will need: two long-handled spoons, roasting pan, 1-quart Mason jar, salad bowl.

1. Peel
- 1 clove garlic

2. Put the garlic in a 1-quart mason jar with
- 2 cups salad oil

3. Cover jar and store in refrigerator at least 1 hour.
4. Throw garlic away and use ¼ cup of the oil to pop some popcorn. You will need
- 1½ cups popped corn

5. Set the popped corn aside.
6. Add to the jar of oil
- 1 cup vinegar
- 1 teaspoon dry mustard
- 2 teaspoons sugar
- 2 teaspoons salt
- ½ teaspoon pepper

7. Put lid on jar and shake vigorously. Store in refrigerator until needed.
8. Wash, drain, and break into pieces
- 1 10-oz. package of fresh spinach

9. Place spinach in large salad bowl.

10. Shake the salad dressing again and pour ¼ cup over spinach. Save the rest in refrigerator for other salads.

11. Add to spinach

- 1½ cups popped corn
- ¼ cup grated Parmesan cheese

12. With a long-handled wooden spoon or fork in each hand, work from the outside of the salad bowl toward the center. Lift the spinach and drop again into bowl. Count at least 200 strokes.

Back-To-School Time

POPCORN APPLE FOR THE TEACHER

This may be the biggest apple any teacher has ever received.

Non-food items you will need: two long-handled spoons, roasting pan, heavy pan, large bowl, plastic wrap or cellophane, green crepe paper (optional), waxed paper.

1. Read "Testing the Syrup for Sugared Popcorn Recipes," in Chapter 3.
2. Read "Mixing the Syrup (or Butter) Through Your Popped Corn," in Chapter 3.
3. Heat in a 200° oven while fixing other ingredients

- 5 quarts (20 cups) popped corn

4. Measure into a heavy pan (such as a cast-iron pressure cooker)

- 2 cups sugar
- 1 6-oz. can frozen apple juice concentrate
- ¾ cup water
- ½ cup light corn syrup
- 2 teaspoons lemon juice
- 2 teaspoons red food coloring

5. Cook over medium high heat to firm ball stage, stirring frequently.
6. Pour syrup over popped corn and mix well.
7. Fill a large bowl with water in which to rinse your hands as you work.
8. Mold into one large ball, indented at the top, to resemble a giant apple.

9. Set on waxed paper to harden.

10. When dry, wrap in clear plastic wrap or red cellophane.

11. If desired, cut a leaf from green crepe paper and place on top.

APRICOT POPCORN BALLS

Dried apricots add both nutrition and variety to your lunch box dessert.

Non-food items you will need: two long-handled spoons, roasting pan, heavy pan, large bowl.

1. Read "Testing the Syrup for Sugared Popcorn Recipes," in Chapter 3.
2. Read "Mixing the Syrup (or Butter) Through Your Popped Corn," in Chapter 3.
3. Heat in a 200° oven while fixing other ingredients

- 2½ quarts (10 cups) popped corn

4. Cut into small pieces and set aside

- 1 cup dried apricots

5. Measure into a heavy pan (such as a cast-iron pressure cooker)
- 1 cup sugar
- ¼ cup light corn syrup
- ¼ cup water

6. Cook over medium high heat to firm ball stage, stirring frequently.
7. Mix apricots with popped corn.
8. Pour syrup over popped corn and mix well.
9. Fill a large bowl with water in which to rinse your hands as you work.
10. Mold popcorn into balls.

Yield: 8 balls

Rosh Hashanah

POPCORN TAIGLACH

Jewish people throughout the world celebrate their New Year, Rosh Hashanah, by eating foods sweetened with honey. This popcorn recipe is an adaptation of a favorite Jewish pastry called taiglach.

Non-food items you will need: two long-handled spoons, roasting pan, heavy pan, waxed paper.

1. Read "Testing the Syrup for Sugared Popcorn Recipes," in Chapter 3.
2. Read "Mixing the Syrup (or Butter) Through Your Popped Corn," in Chapter 3.
3. Heat in a 200° oven while fixing other ingredients

- 3 quarts (12 cups) popped corn

4. Measure into a heavy pan (such as a cast-iron pressure cooker)
- 1 cup honey
- 1 cup light corn syrup
- 1 tablespoon butter
- 1 teaspoon vinegar
- ¼ teaspoon salt
- 1 teaspoon ginger

5. Cook over medium high heat to firm ball stage, stirring frequently.
6. Pour syrup over popped corn and mix well.
7. Set popcorn on waxed paper to harden.

8. Break into chunks.

Yield: 10–12 servings

September Birthday Treat

SUGARY MAPLE POPPERS

Instead of the usual birthday cake, you might like to try this idea for a change. Serve each guest a round ball of vanilla ice cream rolled in coconut with a birthday candle blazing from the top. (These can be made several days in advance and stored between layers of aluminum foil in your freezer.) And give each guest an individual nut cup filled with hot fudge syrup to pour on top of the ice cream. With these sundaes you'll enjoy sugary maple poppers—a rich, cooky-like popcorn treat.

Non-food items you will need: two long-handled spoons, roasting pan, heavy pan, large bowl, birthday candles, nut cups.

1. Read "Mixing the Syrup (or Butter) Through Your Popped Corn," in Chapter 3.
2. Measure into a large pan (but do not pre-heat in the oven)

- 2½ cups popped corn
- ¼ cup coconut
- ¼ cup broken pecans
- grated rind from 1 orange

3. Measure into a heavy pan (such as a cast-iron pressure cooker)

- 2 tablespoons butter
- 1 cup brown sugar, firmly packed
- ¼ cup evaporated milk

4. Place over medium high heat and bring to a vigorous boil, stirring constantly.

5. Boil 3 minutes, stirring constantly, and remove from stove.

6. Add ¼ teaspoon maple flavoring.

7. Pour syrup over dry ingredients and mix well.

8. Fill a large bowl with water in which to rinse your hands as you work.

9. Quickly mold popcorn into cooky-sized servings and set on waxed paper to dry.

Yield: 20 small poppers

OCTOBER

Columbus Day

PARMESAN POPCORN

In honor of Columbus, this recipe combines a great Italian cheese with the delicious American snack food to which the Indians introduced him.

Non-food items you will need: two long-handled spoons, roasting pan, heavy pan.

1. Read "Mixing the Syrup (or Butter) Through Your Popped Corn," in Chapter 3.

2. Measure into a large pan

- 2 quarts (8 cups) popped corn

3. Melt in a heavy pan over low heat

- ¼ cup (½ stick) butter

4. Pour butter over popped corn and mix as directed, counting 100 strokes.

5. Add

- ½ cup grated Parmesan cheese
- ½ teaspoon salt

6. Mix again, counting 100 more strokes.

Yield: 6–8 servings

Halloween

MOLASSES CAT LOLLIPOPS

The flat shape of these cats makes them easier to eat than round popcorn balls. First you make the candied popcorn shapes; then you decorate them as cats.

Non-food items you will need: two long-handled spoons, roasting pan, heavy pan, tuna fish or flat pineapple can, non-stick coating, large bowl, wooden skewers or popsicle sticks, scissors, black pipe cleaners, waxed paper.

Molasses Popcorn
1. Read "Testing the Syrup for Sugared Popcorn Recipes," in Chapter 3.
2. Read "Mixing the Syrup (or Butter) Through Your Popped Corn," in Chapter 3.
3. Heat in a 200° oven while fixing other ingredients

   • 3 quarts (12 cups) popped corn

4. Measure into a heavy pan (such as a cast-iron pressure cooker)
   • 1½ cups sugar
   • ¾ cup molasses
   • ⅓ cup water
   • 1 tablespoon vinegar
   • ¼ teaspoon salt

5. Cook over medium high heat to firm ball stage, stirring frequently.
6. Remove from stove and stir in

   • 2 tablespoons butter

7. Pour syrup over popped corn and mix well.

8. Spray a clean tuna fish can or flat pineapple ring can with non-stick coating.

9. Fill a large bowl with water in which to rinse your hands as you work.

10. Press popcorn into tuna fish or pineapple can and let harden 1–2 minutes.

11. Gently remove popcorn from can with a sharp knife and set on waxed paper to dry.

Yield: 8–10 popcorn discs (depending upon how you filled the cans)

Making the Cats

1. Assemble on a working table

- 8–10 wooden skewers or popsicle sticks
- scissors
- 20 black pipe cleaners, thinnest width
- colored gumdrops

2. Insert a wooden skewer in each popcorn disc to make a lollipop.

3. Cut green gumdrops with scissors and make eyes for cats.

4. Make noses with whole gumdrops.

5. Make ears with black gumdrops or with black pipe cleaners which have been cut and bent.

6. Cut pipe cleaners for whiskers and insert in place.

CREAMY ORANGE WITCHES

These friendly witches and warlocks will please young trick-or-treaters. This recipe makes about 8 witches, depending upon how tightly you pack the popcorn in the cones and how big you make the witches' heads. You can make more witches with this recipe—18 or 20—if you do not put popcorn inside the cones. However, the hats will be more fragile.

First make the candied popcorn and put it in the cones. Then decorate the popcorn to resemble witches.

Non-food items you will need: two long-handled spoons, roasting pan, heavy pan, large bowl, construction paper or cardboard, scissors, compass, pencil, straight pins, waxed paper.

Creamy Orange Popcorn

1. Read "Testing the Syrup for Sugared Popcorn Recipes," in Chapter 3.

2. Read "Mixing the Syrup (or Butter) Through Your Popped Corn," in Chapter 3.

3. Heat in a 200° oven while fixing other ingredients

- 5 quarts (20 cups) popped corn

4. Measure into a heavy pan (such as a cast-iron pressure cooker)

- 2 cups sugar
- ⅔ cup evaporated milk
- 2 tablespoons light corn syrup
- grated rind from 1 orange
- 6 drops orange food coloring

5. Cook over medium *low* heat to firm ball stage, stirring constantly. (This recipe burns very easily. If brown spots begin to form, pour the syrup immediately through a strainer into a clean pan and continue cooking.)

6. Remove from heat and stir in

- 2 tablespoons butter

7. Pour syrup over popped corn and mix well.

8. Fill a large bowl with water in which to rinse your hands as you work.

9. Fill approximately 8 pointed ice cream cones (dark brown) with candied popcorn, rounding the tops like scoops of ice cream. Make the "scoops" as even as possible since they will be the heads for your witches and warlocks.

10. Turn the cones upside down on waxed paper to harden, flattening the popcorn slightly to prevent rolling.

Making the Witches

1. Assemble on a working table

- construction paper or cardboard the same color as cones
- thin licorice strips
- gumdrops
- scissors
- compass

2. Cut lengths of licorice strips for hair of witches and warlocks and moustaches of warlocks. Attach with straight pins or "glue" made from marshmallows and butter melted together in top of double boiler.

3. Cut red gumdrops for noses. Cut other gumdrops for eyes and mouths.

4. Use compass to draw brims of hats on construction paper.

120

Brims should be shaped like doughnuts with the holes about the same size as the widest part of ice cream cones. The outer edges of "doughnuts" should extend about 1 inch farther than the hole all around the circle.

5. Cut brims and slip down points of cones to complete hats.

October Birthday Treat

POPCORN SCARECROWS

These cheerful scarecrows make excellent favors for an October birthday party. They are made in two steps—first the peanut butter popcorn balls and then the rest of the scarecrow bodies. If you enjoy peanut butter, you'll be crazy about this popcorn recipe, which is as easy as it is delicious.

Non-food items you will need: two long-handled spoons, roasting pan, heavy pan, large bowl, dowels, paper cups filled with sand, dirt, or modeling clay, crepe paper (green, yellow, and at least one other color), scissors, glue, pipe cleaners, thin wire.

The Peanut Butter Popcorn Balls
1. Read ·"Mixing the Syrup (or Butter) Through Your Popped Corn," in Chapter 3.
2. Heat in a 200° oven while fixing other ingredients

 • 3 quarts (12 cups) popped corn

3. Measure into a heavy pan (such as a cast-iron pressure cooker)
 • 1 cup sugar
 • 1 cup light corn syrup

4. Bring to vigorous boil and cook 30 seconds, stirring constantly.
5. Remove from stove and add

 • 1 cup peanut butter (creamy or chunk style)
 • 1 teaspoon vanilla

6. Stir briskly with spoon until smooth.

7. Pour syrup over popped corn and mix well.

8. Fill a large bowl with water in which to rinse your hands as you work.

9. Shape popcorn into balls.

Yield: 10 balls

Assemble on a working table

- 10 peanut butter popcorn balls
- 10 thin dowels 8½ inches long
- 10 thin dowels 6 inches long
- 10 paper cups filled with sand, dirt, or modeling clay
- gumdrops for faces
- crepe paper (green, yellow, and at least one other color)
- scissors
- glue
- pipe cleaners
- thin wire

The Coat

1. Fold a piece of colored crepe paper and cut a coat as shown. Glue along dotted lines.

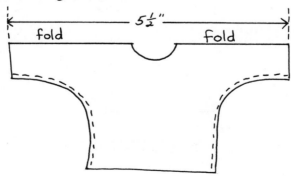

2. Slip a 6-inch dowel through the sleeves of coat as shown.

3. Cut fringe from yellow crepe paper and glue to each end of dowel to resemble straw.

4. Stick an 8½-inch dowel into a popcorn ball.

5. Slip the opposite end of the dowel through the neck of the coat into a paper cup filled with sand, dirt, or clay.

6. Attach the two dowels at right angles at the neck with pipe cleaner.

The Hat

1. Measure a piece of crepe paper around the circumference of the popcorn ball, allowing an extra half-inch overlap for gluing.

2. Cut the crepe paper strip the length of the popcorn measurement and 4 inches wide.

3. Fold a cuff along the long edge of the crepe paper as shown.

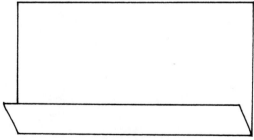

4. Glue the overlap on the crepe paper strip where dotted line is shown.

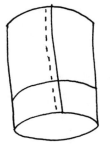

5. Fit the crepe paper on the popcorn head of the scarecrow. Gather at the top with wire.

6. Cut a pompon fringe on the top of the scarecrow hat.

7. Make a face for the scarecrow by cutting gumdrops with scissors.

CORNZAPOPPIN'!

The Stand

1. Glue green crepe paper fringe around base of paper cup.

Yield: 10 scarecrows

NOVEMBER

Veterans Day

HICKORY-SMOKED POPCORN

Hickory salt adds a hearty, outdoors flavor to buttered popcorn.

Non-food items you will need: two long-handled spoons, roasting pan, heavy pan.

1. Read "Mixing the Syrup (or Butter) Through Your Popped Corn," in Chapter 3.
2. Measure into a large pan

- 2½ quarts (10 cups) popped corn

3. Melt in a heavy pan over low heat

- ¼ cup (½ stick) butter

4. Remove from stove and stir in

- ½ teaspoon hickory-smoked salt

5. Pour butter over popped corn and mix well.

Yield: 8–10 servings

Thanksgiving

CORNUCOPIA CENTERPIECE

Among the things we should be grateful for on Thanksgiving is popcorn, which we were taught about by the Indians who came to the first Thanksgiving feast. A fitting symbol of our gratitude for this and the other wonderful foods grown in America is a cornucopia (horn of plenty) made of popcorn.

These instructions are for a very large cornucopia—one big enough for a banquet-sized table. To make a smaller one, use a plastic bottle measuring about 4 inches at the base and cut the popcorn recipe in half. Better still, find a banana squash the shape you would like your cornucopia to be, and use it for your form.

To make your cornucopia you must first prepare your form and then make your popcorn to cover it. Covering the base with popcorn is a difficult operation, and you may want to get a friend to help you with that part (or all) of the job.

Non-food items you will need: two long-handled spoons, roasting pan, 1-gallon plastic bottle with handle, sharp knife, newspapers, scissors, string, aluminum foil, non-stick coating, heavy pan, large bowl.

The Form
1. Find a 1-gallon plastic bottle with a handle, such as a bleach bottle or a distilled water bottle. Although you will

cut off the handle, the neck on such a bottle is graceful and appropriate for a cornucopia because it is long and slightly to one side.

2. With a sharp knife cut the handle off.

3. Remove the lid from the bottle.

4. Fold several thicknesses of newspaper into a strip about 1 inch wide and stuff the paper into the neck of the bottle to elongate it 3 or 4 inches.

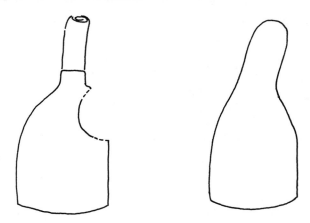

5. Wrap the newspaper extension of the bottle with other newspaper strips and tie them with string for added support. The resulting shape should look like a cornucopia standing upright.

6. Wrap the form completely with aluminum foil.

7. Spray the foil with non-stick coating and then apply another coat of butter or cooking grease.

Old-Fashioned Molasses Popcorn

1. Read "Testing the Syrup for Sugared Popcorn Recipes," in Chapter 3.

2. Read "Mixing the Syrup (or Butter) Through Your Popped Corn," in Chapter 3.

3. Heat in a 200° oven while fixing other ingredients

- 6 quarts (12 cups) popped corn

4. Measure into a heavy pan (such as a cast-iron pressure cooker)

- 2 cups molasses
- 1 cup brown sugar, firmly packed

5. Cook over medium high heat to firm ball stage, stirring occasionally.

6. Remove from heat and stir in

- 4 tablespoons butter

7. Pour syrup over popped corn and mix well.

Covering the Form with Popcorn

1. Fill a large bowl with water in which to rinse your hands as you work.

2. Keep at your side for use as you work

- scissors
- heavy string
- several long sheets of aluminum foil which have been sprayed with non-stick coating and then buttered or greased

3. With bottle still standing upright, mold popcorn against the form from the bottom up.

4. When you get a coat of popcorn all around the base and about three or four inches up, hold it in place by wrapping a layer of foil around it and tying the foil in place with string. (Buttered side of foil against the popcorn.)

5. Continue the process until all the form is covered first with popcorn, then foil, and last string, as shown. If string makes indentations, do not worry, because original cornucopias were irregularly shaped rams' horns.

6. Because the popcorn is applied in a much thinner layer than the popcorn for the hollow Easter basket described earlier, the cornucopia will be much more fragile. You must therefore let it dry completely before you remove it from the form—about 1 week.

7. Cut the string and carefully remove the outside layer of foil.

8. Feel the popcorn to make certain it is dry all over.

9. Lift the popcorn cornucopia carefully from the form, removing any pieces of foil that may stick to it.

10. Set the cornucopia on its side and fill with grapes, bananas, oranges, nuts, etc. as a Thanksgiving centerpiece.

November Birthday Treat

POPMEN FROM OUTER SPACE

These green-eared visitors from outer space will delight your birthday party guests. They are very easy to assemble, but first you must make the popcorn and mold it into two different shapes—balls and discs.

Because this candied popcorn may harden before you are able to make all twenty shapes, try to get one or two people to help you form them. If you must work alone, prepare the candied popcorn in two separate batches.

Non-food items you will need: two long-handled spoons, roasting pan, heavy pan, tuna fish or pineapple can, non-stick coating, large bowl, green pipe cleaners, popsicle sticks, scissors, waxed paper.

Spicy Orange Popcorn
1. Read "Testing the Syrup for Sugared Popcorn Recipes," in Chapter 3.
2. Read "Mixing the Syrup (or Butter) Through Your Popped Corn," in Chapter 3.
3. Heat in a 200° oven while fixing other ingredients

- 6 quarts (24 cups) popped corn

4. Measure into a heavy pan (such as a cast-iron pressure cooker)
- 3½ cups sugar
- 1 cup light corn syrup
- ½ cup red cinnamon candies
- 2 teaspoons lemon juice

134

- 1 cup orange juice
- grated peel from 2 oranges
- ½ teaspoon salt

5. Cook to firm ball stage, stirring occasionally.

6. Remove from heat and stir in

- ¼ cup (½ stick) butter

7. Pour syrup over popped corn and mix well.

8. Spray a clean, empty tuna fish or flat pineapple can with non-stick coating.

9. Fill a large bowl with water in which to rinse your hands as you work.

10. Make 10 popcorn discs by pressing half the popcorn into the tuna fish can. Let harden for 30 seconds or so and set on waxed paper to dry.

11. Make 10 popcorn balls by shaping half the popcorn into balls.

The Popmen

1. Assemble on a working table

- 10 popcorn balls
- 10 popcorn discs
- 20 green pipe cleaners (6–8 inches long)
- 10 popsicle sticks
- scissors
- green gumdrops

2. Insert one end of a popsicle stick in a popcorn ball, the other end in the center of the flat end of a popcorn disc.

3. Wrap the center of a pipe cleaner around the popsicle stick to make two arms.

4. Coil another pipe cleaner and stick it on popcorn ball for antenna.

5. Use whole gumdrops for green ears and a green nose.

6. Cut gumdrops with scissors for eyes and mouth.

Yield: 10 popmen

DECEMBER

Christmas

Popcorn has established itself as a Christmas tradition in nearly every American home. Here are several Christmas popcorn recipes, some new and some old, to make the holidays more festive at your house.

POPCORN "GINGERBREAD" HOUSE

Non-food items you will need: two long-handled spoons, roasting pan, heavy cardboard, ruler, pencil, scissors, scotch or masking tape, aluminum foil, non-stick coating, cooky sheet, heavy pan, large bowl, double boiler, hand mixer, saucepan.

Making the House
1. Follow instructions for popcorn log cabin (see Lincoln's Birthday, pp. 36-40).
2. To add December "snow," cover the roof of house and chimney with seven-minute icing or marshmallow cream frosting; recipes below.
3. Make doors and windows with square candies or cake decorator and icing.
4. Decorate roof and exterior walls with brightly colored candies of many kinds.

Seven-Minute Icing
1. Put water in bottom half of double boiler and place on stove to boil.

2. Measure into top of double boiler

- 1 unbeaten egg white
- ⅞ cup sugar
- 3 tablespoons water

3. Put top of double boiler over boiling water.

4. Beat egg white mixture 7 minutes with hand mixer as it cooks.

5. Remove from stove and add

- ½ teaspoon vanilla

6. Spread on roof of house.

Marshmallow Cream Frosting

1. Measure into a saucepan and bring to a fast boil

- ¾ cup sugar
- ¼ cup milk

2. Boil for five minutes, stirring constantly.

3. Place water in bottom half of double boiler and bring to a boil.

4. In top half of double boiler measure

- 2 tablespoons hot water
- 2 tablespoons marshmallow cream
  (or 6 large marshmallows)
- ½ teaspoon vanilla

5. Stir until smooth.

6. Gradually add milk and sugar mixture to marshmallow mixture, stirring constantly.

7. When cool, spread on roof of house.

POPCORN CHRISTMAS WREATHS

Make big ones to give as presents to neighbors; keep individual ones on hand for Christmas visitors at your house.

Non-food items you will need: two long-handled spoons, roasting pan, ring-shaped gelatin molds—both individual and family size, aluminum foil, non-stick coating, heavy pan, large bowl, cellophane, red satin ribbon, waxed paper.

1. Line a 1½-quart ring-shaped gelatin mold with aluminum foil; spray with non-stick coating.
2. Spray individual gelatin ring molds with non-stick coating.
3. Use green candied popcorn recipes for St. Patrick's Day, pp. 52-53.
4. Fill a large bowl with water in which to rinse your hands as you work.
5. Press candied popcorn inside ring molds.
6. Let harden 30 seconds or longer.
7. Gently remove popcorn from molds and set on waxed paper.
8. Decorate while still warm with gumdrops, broken pieces of peppermint candy, miniature (2-inch long) candy canes, if desired.
9. Wrap wreaths in cellophane and tie with red satin ribbon.

Yield: 1 large wreath and twenty small wreaths.

POPCORN STARS

Non-food items you will need: two long-handled spoons, roasting pan, heavy pan, star-shaped individual gelatin molds or cooky cutters, non-stick coating, large bowl, waxed paper.

1. Read "Testing the Syrup for Sugared Popcorn Recipes," in Chapter 3.
2. Read "Mixing the Syrup (or Butter) Through Your Popped Corn," in Chapter 3.
3. Cut into small pieces and set aside

- ½ cup candied grapefruit peel
- ½ cup candied lemon peel
- ½ cup candied orange peel

4. Heat in a 200° oven while fixing other ingredients

- 5 quarts (20 cups) popped corn

5. Measure into a heavy pan (such as a cast-iron pressure cooker)

- 2 cups sugar
- ½ cup light corn syrup
- ½ cup water

6. Cook to soft ball stage, stirring frequently.
7. Remove from heat and add

- 1 tablespoon butter
- candied fruit peels

8. Pour syrup over popped corn and mix well.
9. Spray star-shaped individual gelatin molds or cooky cutters with non-stick coating.

10. Fill a large bowl with water in which to rinse your hands as you work.

11. Press popcorn into molds and let harden 10–30 seconds.

12. Remove gently with sharp knife and set on waxed paper to dry.

Yield: 20 small stars

SURPRISE SNOWBALLS

For an attractive arrangement, pile these on a silver platter and circle them with holly.

Non-food items you will need: two long-handled spoons, roasting pan, double boiler, large bowl.

1. Read "Testing the Syrup for Sugared Popcorn Recipes," in Chapter 3.
2. Read "Mixing the Syrup (or Butter) Through Your Popped Corn," in Chapter 3.
3. Heat in 200° oven while fixing other ingredients

- 3 quarts (12 cups) popped corn

4. Count and set aside

- 12 chocolate malted milk balls

5. Put water in bottom half of double boiler and place on stove to boil.
6. Measure into top half of double boiler

- 1 lb. miniature marshmallows
- ¼ cup (½ stick) butter

7. Melt marshmallows and butter over boiling water in double boiler, stirring constantly.
8. Remove from stove and add

- 1 teaspoon vanilla

9. Pour syrup over popped corn and mix well.
10. Fill a large bowl with water in which to rinse your hands as you work.
11. Form popcorn into balls around malted milk balls.
12. Roll in coconut.

Yield: 12 small snowballs

December Birthday Centerpiece

POPCORN SNOWMEN

Non-food items you will need: two long-handled spoons, roasting pan, double boiler, large bowl, heavy pan, brandy snifters, black felt or pompons, water-soluble glue, doll hats and scarves, holly (optional).

1. Assemble on working table

- 3 brandy snifters, graduated sizes
- 3 large snowballs, graduated sizes, for heads (recipe above, p. 145)
- black felt circles or black pompons for buttons
- water-soluble glue
- doll hats and scarves
- orange gumdrops
- raisins or semi-sweet chocolate pieces
- sugared popcorn (July 4th recipe)

2. Paste felt or pompon "buttons" down fronts of brandy snifters.

3. Cut orange gumdrops for noses. (Stick to snowballs with straight pins, or make edible glue by melting marshmallows and butter together in top of double boiler.)

4. Make eyes and mouths with raisins or chocolate pieces.

5. Fill brandy snifters with sugared popcorn.

6. Put heads on snowmen.

7. Add hats, scarves.

8. Put small twigs of holly around bases of brandy snifters, if desired.

144

New Year's Eve

MIDNIGHT POPCORN CLOCKS

These clocks say midnight—popcorn time.

Non-food items you will need: two long-handled spoons, roasting pan, heavy pan, flat cake pans (round and square), non-stick coating, dowels or popsicle sticks, styrofoam circle, serpentine (streamers), confetti, waxed paper.

Maple Popcorn for the Clocks
1. Read "Testing the Syrup for Sugared Popcorn Recipes," in Chapter 3.
2. Read "Mixing the Syrup (or Butter) Through Your Popped Corn," in Chapter 3.
3. Heat in a 200° oven while fixing other ingredients

- 6 quarts (24 cups) popped corn

4. Measure into a heavy pan (such as a cast-iron pressure cooker)
- 2 cups sugar
- 1 cup brown sugar, firmly packed
- ¾ cup light corn syrup
- 1 cup water
- 1 teaspoon vinegar

5. Cook to firm ball stage, stirring frequently.
6. Remove from heat and stir in

- 2 tablespoons butter
- 1 teaspoon maple flavoring

7. Pour syrup over popped corn and mix well.

8. Spray a variety of flat cake pans (both round and square) with non-stick coating.

9. Press the popcorn into the pans and let harden for 3–4 minutes.

10. Remove popcorn gently with sharp knife and set on waxed paper to harden.

Making the Clocks

1. Put a popsicle stick or strong dowel in a narrow edge of each clock.

2. Break dowels so they are different lengths.

3. Set flat round candies around the sides of each circle or square to resemble the numbers on a clock.

4. With lengths of licorice twists or stick candy, make a long hand and short hand on each clock, pointing to one minute before midnight.

5. Insert the other ends of the dowels in a large circle of styrofoam so that clocks face in different directions at different heights.

6. Drape serpentine around the clocks and dribble confetti over all.

147

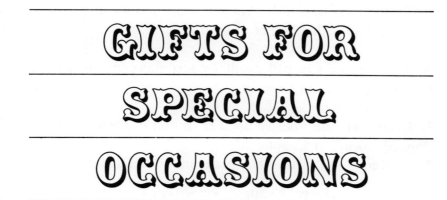

GIFTS FOR SPECIAL OCCASIONS

Get Well Treat

CINNAMON-SUGAR POPCORN

Know someone who is ill? Make a short and sweet visit to a shut-in friend with a bag of this delicious treat.

Non-food items you will need: 1-quart saucepan, two long-handled spoons, roasting pan.

1. Read "Mixing the Syrup (or Butter) Through Your Popped Corn," in Chapter 3.
2. Heat in a 200° oven while fixing other ingredients

- 3 quarts (12 cups) popped corn

3. Mix together in a bowl

- ½ cup sugar
- 1 tablespoon cinnamon

4. Melt in a saucepan over low heat

- ½ cup (1 stick) butter

5. Pour butter over popped corn and count 100 strokes.
6. Add cinnamon sugar and count 100 more strokes.
Note: This recipe is not suitable for forming into balls or other shapes.

Going-Away Present

BAKED CARAMEL CORN

Is someone you know going away? You will be remembered fondly if you say goodbye with a bag of baked caramel corn.

Non-food items you will need: two long-handled spoons, roasting pan, heavy pan.

1. Read "Mixing the Syrup (or Butter) Through Your Popped Corn," in Chapter 3.
2. In a large roasting pan measure

- 6 quarts (24 cups) popped corn

3. Measure into a heavy pan (such as a cast-iron pressure cooker)

- 1 cup (2 sticks) butter cut into 8 or more chunks
- 2 cups brown sugar, firmly packed
- ½ cup light corn syrup
- 1 teaspoon salt
- 2 cups raw peanuts

4. Bring to a vigorous boil, stirring constantly.
5. Cook 2 minutes over medium heat.
6. Remove from heat and add

- ½ teaspoon baking soda
- 1 teaspoon vanilla

7. Pour syrup over popped corn, mixing well.
8. Bake in 250° oven for 1 hour, stirring well every 15 minutes. An electric roaster oven with removable top is ideal

151

for baking because popcorn is easy to stir. Do not overload pan.

9. Remove popcorn from oven and let cool. Break into chunks.

Note: This recipe is not suitable for forming into balls or other shapes.

Welcome-To-The-Neighborhood Gift

POPCORN PEANUT CLUSTERS

Has a new family moved into your neighborhood recently? Welcome them with a platter of popcorn peanut clusters.

Non-food items you will need: two long-handled spoons, roasting pan, double boiler, waxed paper.

1. Read "Mixing the Syrup (or Butter) Through Your Popped Corn," in Chapter 3.

2. Heat in a 200° oven while fixing other ingredients

- 4 quarts (16 cups) popped corn

3. Place water in bottom half of double boiler and put on stove.

4. When water boils, turn heat down immediately to simmer. Do not let water boil under chocolate.

5. In top half of double boiler measure

- 2 pounds (32 ozs.) of sweet dipping chocolate
- 1 tablespoon light corn syrup

6. Place top half of double boiler on stove, stirring as chocolate melts.

7. Mix into popcorn

- 1 cup unsalted peanuts

8. Remove chocolate from stove and pour over popcorn and peanuts, mixing well.

9. Drop mixture by spoonfuls onto waxed paper to dry.

153

INDEX

INDEX

158